D0805665

sisters and brothers

HOW MUCH DO YOU REALLY KNOW ABOUT SIBLINGS?
TAKE THIS QUIZ TO TEST YOUR SIB SMARTS.

True or False?

1 There is some evidence that oldest children tend to be smarter than their younger siblings.

2 Siblings always have similar personalities.

3 Half siblings are brothers or sisters who share one biological parent.

4 Most U.S. presidents were born last in their families.

5 It's rare for American kids to have stepbrothers or stepsisters.

Answer key:

(1) True. The older brothers in one study had IQs that were slightly higher on average than their younger brothers. And that's not the only effect your birth order can have on you. Learn more in Chapters One and Two. **(2)** False. Not necessarily. Siblings often try hard to be as different as possible from each other—and they usually succeed. See why in Chapter One. **(3)** True. Half siblings are produced when a parent has children with two different partners. Read more in Chapter Two. **(4)** False. Most U.S. presidents have been firstborns or firstborn boys in their families. Read more in Chapter Two. **(5)** False. Today, six out of ten kids in the United States live in a stepfamily at one point in their lives. Read about the lives of these kids and others in Chapter Two.

Chapter two: The information on page 29 is from the U.S. Department of State. The information on page 30 is from the Center for Adoption Support and Education, Inc. The information on page 38 is from the Child Welfare Information Gateway. The information on page 39 is from FosterClub. **Jonathan's story** was originally published in "My Brother Has Down Syndrome," by Heather Holliday, in *Scholastic Choices*, October 2002. The information on page 59 is from the U.S. Census Bureau. The information on page 68 is from the National Stepfamily Resource Center and the Stepfamily Foundation. **Amy and Ashly's story** was originally published in "Twice as Nice," by Denise Rinaldo, in *Scholastic Choices*, May 2003. **Chapter three:** Some material in this chapter was originally published in "I Can't Stand My Sister!" by Darcy Lockman, *Scholastic Choices*, September 2001, and "The Sibling Saga," by Sean Price, *Scholastic Choices*, February/March 2006.

Photographs © 2008: age fotostock: 40 (Photodisc), 21 (Somos); Alamy Images: 34 (Bubbles Photolibrary), 15 (Andrew Paterson), 5, 9 (Photofusion Picture Library); Corbis Images: 77 (Keith Bedford/Reuters), 39 (Bettmann), 31 bottom (Bohemian Nomad Picturemakers), 50 (Alessandro Della Valle/Keystone/epa), 33 (David P. Hall), 17 (Claudia Hehr/zefa), 25 (Michael A. Keller/zefa), 22 (Darren Modricker), 19 bottom (Anthony Redpath), 35 (Sandra Seckinger/zefa), 69 (Marc Serota/Reuters); Getty Images: 24, 51 (Ewa Ahlin), 58 bottom, 58 top (Tony Anderson), 76 (Ira Block), 41 (Chris Clinton), 100 (David Deas), 96 (Gustavo Di Mario), 97, 98 (DreamPictures), 4, 31 top (Blasius Erlinger), 6 (Frank Herholdt), 67 (Andrew Hetherington), 43 (Chistina Kennedy), 48, 53 (Ryan McVay), 18 (Patrick Molnar), 84 (Gala Narezo), 78, 79, 81, 86, 89 (Erin Patrice O'Brien), 70 bottom, 70 top (Shalom Ormsby), 71 (Bill Reitzel/Plush Studios), 14 (Chad Riley), 19 top (Richard Schultz), 46 (Julia Smith), 91 (Penny Tweedie), 94 (Rachel Weill), 64 (David Young-Wolff), 63 (Gale Zucker); JupiterImages/Dave & Les Jacobs: 87; Masterfile/Edward Pond: 13; Monty Stilson: cover; PhotoEdit/Bill Aron: 10; Retna Ltd./Walter McBride: 56; Still Media/Brian Bailey: 32; Superstock, Inc./Creatas: 45.

Cover design: Marie O'Neill
Book production: The Design Lab
CHOICES editor: Bob Hugel

Library of Congress Cataloging-in-Publication Data
Winchester, Elizabeth.
 Sisters and brothers : the ultimate guide to understanding your
siblings and yourself / Elizabeth Siris Winchester.
    p. cm.
 Includes bibliographical references and index.
 ISBN-13: 978-0-531-13870-0 (lib. bdg.)   978-0-531-20528-0 (pbk.)
 ISBN-10: 0-531-13870-4 (lib. bdg.)   0-531-20528-2 (pbk.)
 1. Brothers and sisters. 2. Family. 3. Interpersonal relations.
 I.Title.
 HQ759.96.W56 2008
 306.875'3—dc22   2007051871

1 2 3 4 5 6 7 8 9 10 R 17 16 15 14 13 12 11 10 09 08

CHOICES™

The ultimate guide to
understanding your
siblings and yourself

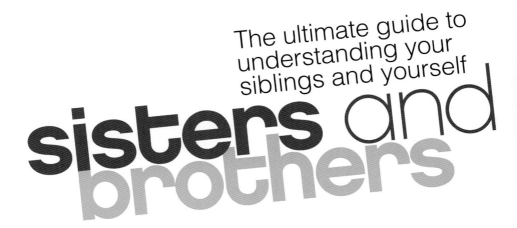

sisters and brothers

Elizabeth Siris Winchester

Franklin Watts®

AN IMPRINT OF SCHOLASTIC INC.
NEW YORK • TORONTO • LONDON • AUCKLAND • SYDNEY
MEXICO CITY • NEW DELHI • HONG KONG
DANBURY, CONNECTICUT

family ties

family ties

"NO ONE CAN TELL WE ARE SIBLINGS."

*People always say that my older brother Andrew and I have similar noses, but other than that no one can tell we are **siblings**. I have dark brown hair. His hair is red. We have different skin tones. Our **personalities** are different too. As a kid, I always liked to act and sing, and my brother was quieter. He didn't have many friends because he was always too shy to talk to people. He would just stay at home and read and play games.*

—Jenny, 15

How do you get along with your siblings? Do you and your brother seem to come from different species like Jenny and Andrew? Or are you joined at the hip? Are you good friends, or do you drive each other crazy?

No matter how you answer these questions, one thing is certain: The **relationships** you have with your siblings are among the most important in your life. Friends come and go. Spouses miss the first part of your life; parents miss the last. Siblings are with you the entire way.

The RELATIONSHIPS you have with your SIBLINGS are among the most important in your life.

My sister, Christine, is older than me—but just by seconds. We're twins. We're completely alike. We both have brown hair and hazel eyes, but I'm about two inches taller. We find the same things funny. We enjoy going on the same kinds of trips. I consider us both pretty creative and artsy. We have a passion for music. We always sing together in the car. Most kids grow up relying on their parents, but I had that connection with my sister.

—Joseph, 18

And they are not just there to fight with
or ignore. Siblings actually help to shape our
personalities. From day one, whether we like it or
not, we measure our successes and failures against
theirs. "We share space in the family with them,"
writes Susan Scarf Merrell, author of *The Accidental
Bond*, "we learn from them and teach them, we
divide up parental loyalties with them, we envy them,
admire them, dominate them, hate them, love them."
Along the way, siblings help to make us who we are.

How do they do it? Let's count the ways.

Sibling School

Younger siblings learn all kinds of things from their more enlightened elders: how to master a video game, why they look like a jerk when they wear pants that are too short, when it's best to stay out of Mom's way.

But the real wisdom we get from our siblings doesn't come just from the things they teach us. It comes from the way we **interact** with them. Consider that at age 11, most kids spend one-third of their free hours with their brothers or sisters. That's more time than they spend with anyone else, including friends, parents, or teachers. All those hours of playing, talking, and even fighting can provide a training ground for life. "Sibling relationships are a model that people carry in their heads for how people get along with one another," explains Richard Gallagher, a child and **adolescent psychologist** at the New York University Child Study Center.

"Sibling relationships are a model for how people get along with one another."

That model can affect your friendships for the rest of your life, according to Dr. Ruth Waldbaum, a **psychiatrist** in Manhasset, New York. Siblings who are overly competitive with each other might repeat the behavior with friends. On the other hand, sibs who learn to get along may have an advantage in the outside world. One Canadian study showed that kids who resolved sibling conflict in a productive way at home tended to do the same with classmates at school.

THE SIBLING EFFECT

Dr. Waldbaum offers the following examples for how sibling relationships can affect how we deal with the wider world:

Competitive and jealous siblings might re-enact these struggles with friends. Or they may only feel comfortable with friends who avoid conflict entirely.

Poor relationships between brothers and sisters might color their relationships with the opposite sex.

A person who has had really nurturing relationships with siblings might look for something similar in a friendship or romantic relationship, or just the opposite.

There is no exact formula for how your sibling experiences will affect your relationship choices later in life. But like it or not, there will probably be some effect.

    Sibling relationships may also have an effect
on your romantic life. For one study done in Texas,
researchers put male and female students together
and got them talking. Students who had older
siblings of the opposite sex tended to have more to
say. They were also better liked by their partners. Of
course, as Waldbaum points out, a bad relationship
with a brother or sister can make it hard to be
successful with a future partner.

Not Like Me

To understand another way that siblings influence us, take a look at 15-year-old Jenny, who's quoted at the beginning of this chapter. At first glance, her experience with her brother Andrew seems unlikely. How could two people who share so much be so different from each other? They've grown up in the same house, with the same parents, eating the same food. What happened along the way to turn them into opposites?

Psychologists answer that question with just one word: De-identification. Translated, that means that many people actually work hard to set themselves apart from—or "de-identify" with—their siblings. They adopt different personality traits, different hobbies, and different goals in life. They try to find their own niche.

De-identification serves a couple of important purposes. It helps defuse nasty rivalries between siblings. It also helps everyone in a family win approval. Suppose your older sister plays flute in the city orchestra, consistently wins the lead in the school play, and gets her paintings shown at the local gallery. How can you compete with that? If you want attention, you're better off taking up soccer.

Most parents don't want their kids competing all the time, so they tend to encourage them to be different. "Christine," they'll say, "she's always been the artistic one. Amy is the athlete." After a while, kids live up to these expectations.

Siblings adopt different personality traits, different hobbies, and different goals in life.

Order in the Family

You have no control over the order in which you and your siblings are born, but it may have a lot of control over you. Everyone feels the effects of **birth order** while they're growing up. Younger siblings are usually surrounded by people who walk, talk, read, and run better than they can. Older siblings often have to cope with chores and homework while their

CLASHINGKIDS

Siblings between the ages of three and seven engage in some kind of conflict at an average of 3.5 times an hour, according to a study by Laurie Kramer of the University of Illinois at Urbana-Champaign as reported in *Time* magazine.

"Most everyone feels the effects of birth order while they're growing up."

brothers and sisters are still playing with Legos. No matter where they stand in the family hierarchy, everyone complains loudly about the injustices— while secretly acknowledging the advantages.

What they may not realize is that the simple fact of their position in the family can have a big influence on their personalities, their relationships, and their career choices. An Austrian psychologist named Alfred Adler first suggested the theory nearly 100 years ago. Children, he said, are constantly competing for love and attention from their parents. Their strategies have a lot to do with their position in the family. Older siblings tend to

1st

2nd BORN

rely on their superior skills and accomplishments. Younger children may have to charm their way into the spotlight by entertaining people.

Kevin Leman, psychologist and author of *The Birth Order Book: Why You Are the Way You Are*,

3rd BORN

claims these strategies mold the lives of siblings long after they leave the home. Firstborns, he writes, "are more highly motivated to achieve than later-borns." According to his theory, later-borns tend to be more rebellious and lean toward creative jobs. (See the profiles in Chapter Two for more.)

who's the
FAVORITE?

According to a *Time* magazine poll, 82 percent of people felt their parents didn't favor one child over another.

   The theory has plenty of critics, who claim that research hasn't clearly shown the differences between firstborns and later-borns. Birth order, after all, is just one of many influences in a person's childhood. People are also shaped by their genes, by their family's income level, by their parents playing favorites, and countless other factors. But Leman, Adler, and others believe looking at birth order can help us understand some of the ways people interact with others.

all in the
family

all in the family

WHAT ROLE DO YOU PLAY IN YOUR FAMILY?

Are you a middle child? Adopted? A step sibling? All of the above? In this chapter, you'll meet eight different types of siblings: adopted, foster, half, middle, oldest, step, twin, and youngest. Only children are there, too. All these categories are listed alphabetically, and for each one, you'll read about a real kid, and get some advice about important issues.

Of course, every sibling's story is unique. If you were born first in your family, that doesn't mean you'll find a kindred spirit in every firstborn you meet. But chances are you'll have something important in common.

After you've looked yourself up, have a look at some other categories and see what it might be like to be in someone else's shoes.

Adopted
SIBS

Eliana's Story

Eliana, 16, says her relationships with her two sisters are no different from most other sibling relationships. She and her 12-year-old sister, Sara, talk about music, fashion, and boys they think are hot. She and her sister Julia, 11, follow baseball together, always rooting for the New York Yankees. Like most siblings, the sisters love each other but have their share of fights. Unlike most siblings, they each have different **biological** parents.

Eliana was adopted from Colombia when she was an infant. Sara joined the family from the same country four years later. Just after Sara arrived, their adoptive mother found out that she was pregnant with Julia.

Eliana has always been comfortable with her place in the family, thanks in part to the fact that her parents don't play favorites. "Julia definitely doesn't get any special treatment," Eliana explains. "My sisters and I are all treated the same." Julia, she says, looks a lot like their mom, but that doesn't make Eliana jealous. She just thinks it's cool that physical traits can be passed on through the generations.

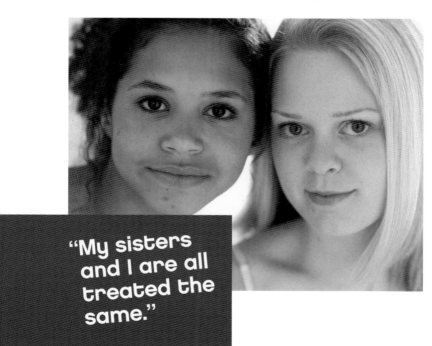

"My sisters and I are all treated the same."

But Eliana also feels grateful to have another adopted sister in the family. As she gets older, she has started to think more about her origins. She wants to meet her biological parents someday and hopes they can answer a few questions about her birth. And she knows that Sara understands what she's going through. "It's just nice to have someone close to home who can relate to how you're feeling," says Eliana.

For now, Eliana confides more in Sara than she does in Julia. But she's convinced that will change as Julia gets older. The fact that they don't share the same biological parents doesn't matter, Eliana says, adding that adopted kids can be just as close to their siblings as kids who are related by blood. "We're not any different," she says, "and we shouldn't be treated any different."

About Adoption

About 150,000 kids are adopted every year in the United States. Many of them live with parents who also have biological children. Is Eliana right when she says that adopted and biological siblings do just fine together? According to the experts, she is. Research shows that adopted and biological siblings don't have big problems adjusting to each other. After all, many kids in mixed families form a bond before they even know what it means to be adopted.

Still, when adopted kids become teenagers, identity may become more of an issue for them. "All teens go through identity issues," says Kim Stevens, co-director of Massachusetts Families for Kids. "That's an age when they're supposed to negotiate how to have an identity separate from Mom and Dad. Adopted kids . . . have to figure out who they are in addition to the family they've grown up in, and they start asking questions about the family they never knew."

TIPS
for Adopted
TEENS

Judy Howell-Wadsworth, an adoptive mother who worked for adoption groups in Minnesota, offers this advice:

TALK ABOUT IT: Share your feelings about being adopted with your parents, siblings, and school counselors.

EXPLORE YOUR HISTORY: If you have questions about your biological parents, see whether you can find the answers.

BE PROUD: Remember that you aren't any less important than a biological sibling. Your adoptive parents chose to adopt you, and that makes your place in the family special.

Every year, about 150,000 kids are adopted in the United States. In 2006, 20,679 of them were born outside the U.S.

adoptions in the
UNITED STATES

Leading countries of origin of orphaned children adopted in the United States in 2006

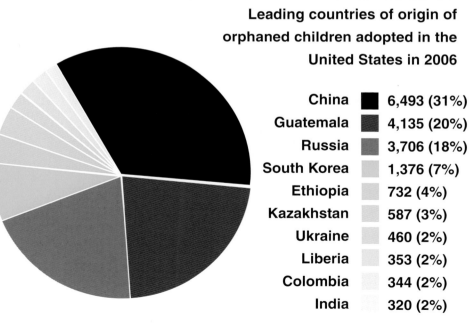

China		6,493 (31%)
Guatemala		4,135 (20%)
Russia		3,706 (18%)
South Korea		1,376 (7%)
Ethiopia		732 (4%)
Kazakhstan		587 (3%)
Ukraine		460 (2%)
Liberia		353 (2%)
Colombia		344 (2%)
India		320 (2%)

FAMOUS
adoptees

Edward Albee, playwright

John J. Audubon, naturalist

Eric Dickerson, NFL running back

Andrew Jackson, seventh U.S. president

Steve Jobs, founder, Apple Computer

Greg Louganis, Olympic diver

Sarah McLachlan, singer

Tom Monaghan, founder, Domino's Pizza

Jim Palmer, major league baseball pitcher

Dave Thomas, founder, Wendy's restaurants

Anthony Williams, mayor of Washington, D.C.

"We're all the same. Someone handpicked us—and that means a lot. That means we were really wanted."

—Actor Malcolm David Kelley
(Walt on ABC's *Lost*)

Foster SIBS

Skye's Story

Skye and her biological brother, James, have traveled a lot together. Four times they've packed their bags and moved from one family to another. Since she was eight years old, Skye has shuttled between her biological family and two different foster families. In each new foster family, she has gotten to know a new set of siblings. And according to Skye, who is now 15, they were often as important to her as James.

In one foster home, Skye and her brother lived with four other kids, each of whom had different biological parents. Three of the kids had been adopted, and the fourth was a foster child. But labels didn't matter much to Skye. "All the kids were the same to me," she explains. "I just treated them all like they were my sister or brother."

The hardest thing about **foster care** for Skye was the fear of being torn from her new siblings. She once became very close to a foster sister. "We were only siblings for two weeks, but we were really close," Skye explains. "We always walked together around the block, rode bikes, and hung out together

with friends." But after two weeks, her foster sister was sent to live with her own biological brothers. She and Skye lost contact. "I still miss her," Skye says. "I miss everything about her."

Since then, Skye has gained more siblings. Her latest move also gave her a promotion, from middle child to oldest. "I like being the oldest," she says, "because I get to do more things than the other kids do, like hang out with my friends without my parents being there and staying out later."

Last fall, Skye and James were adopted by their second set of foster parents. They live with two adopted siblings and two foster siblings. As always, Skye wasted no time getting to know them. It's important for siblings to explore the interests they have in common, she says. She reads to her younger siblings and plays sports with the ones her age. She doesn't want to lose any of them, James or the others. "I treat everyone the same," Skye explains. "We get to know more about each other every day."

> ## "We get to know more about each other every day."

About Foster Kids

Every year, about 200,000 American kids have to leave their homes and enter foster care. For one reason or another—a parent's illness, death, drug addiction, abuse—they can't live at home anymore. The state finds new homes for them with trained and licensed foster parents. Some foster kids go back to their biological parent or parents when the state thinks everyone is ready. Other kids are adopted by their foster parents or someone else.

Foster families often take in more than one kid, so foster kids can find themselves with a wealth of siblings. Many adjust to their new families as Skye did. They make friends quickly and feel at home. Others aren't so lucky. Some feel torn between their new family and their biological family. They may feel guilty for leaving their biological parents or want to return even if they weren't happy there.

Often foster kids are forced to move around and have trouble getting close to new parents and siblings. "The match between foster parents, their children, and the child being placed is so important," says Judy Howell-Wadsworth, who has worked in the foster care system for 27 years. "It must be right in order for the child to totally succeed."

"The match must be right in order for the foster child to totally succeed."

TIPS for foster KIDS

BE TEAMMATES: Think of your foster siblings as allies, not enemies, says Howell-Wadsworth.

LOOK BACK: Realize that your past may affect how you respond in a new situation. If something is upsetting you, stop and ask yourself whether you're reacting to the past or the present.

SPEAK UP: If anything about your foster care placement makes you uncomfortable, talk to your foster parents, guardian, or social worker.

EXPLORE LIFE: Take advantage of the opportunities that your foster family provides. Focus on the things in life you can control, not the things you can't.

TIPS for teens with foster SIBS

BE MINDFUL OF DIFFERENCES: Your foster siblings may have had difficult lives before joining your family, Howell-Wadsworth says. If a foster sib upsets you, try to understand where he is coming from before you react.

BE POSITIVE: Don't criticize a foster sibling's past. Her biological family is part of her history, and she may go back to live with them someday.

COMMUNICATE: Talk to your parents about your feelings. A certain amount of resentment toward a new family member is natural, but your parents can probably help you work through it.

by the
NUMBERS

The number of kids in foster care has been going up since the 1980s. The goal is to get kids adopted or back into their own families as quickly as possible, but it doesn't always happen that way.

About **513,000** U.S. kids were in foster care as of September 2005.

Of these kids, **25 percent** had been in foster care for three years or longer; **42 percent** were in for less than a year.

Fifty-one percent of the kids wanted to return to their original family; **20 percent** hoped to be adopted.

25%

42%

51%

20%

FAMOUS
former foster kids

Cher, singer and actor

Daunte Culpepper, NFL quarterback

James Dean, actor

Ice-T, musician and actor

John Lennon, musician ——————▶

Marilyn Monroe, actor

Alonzo Mourning, NBA center

Eddie Murphy, actor and comedian

Dan O'Brien, Olympic decathlete

Half SIBS

Jamie's Story

Jamie's two older sisters, Vera and Lorin, are his **half siblings**—their mom remarried before Jamie was born. But he insists that's not why they subjected him to a series of life-threatening experiments while they were growing up in Maine. Once, Jamie remembers, Vera and Lorin lowered him to the ground with a sheet from the second floor of their house. "Miraculously, I survived," he says.

Today, at 18, Jamie laughs about his role as "test dummy" for his older sisters' pranks. He says it was all about age and gender, not the fact that he was their half brother. Jamie also has a full sister, Michel, who is three years younger, and he treated her in much the same way his older sisters treated him. "My relationships with all of my sisters are as equal as they can be. There is one significant difference: I had no chance of bossing Vera or Lorin. At least with Michel, I had some chance."

Still, Jamie's half sisters had a mysterious, separate life while they were growing up, and Jamie didn't always like it. Vera and Lorin often disappeared for weekends to see their father. Every now and then, they took off for weeklong trips to Disney World or some other exotic place. The excursions to "kid heaven," as Jamie remembers it, made him boil with envy. Once he blew up at Vera, telling her that he hated her father. "I remember Vera was very hurt," Jamie says.

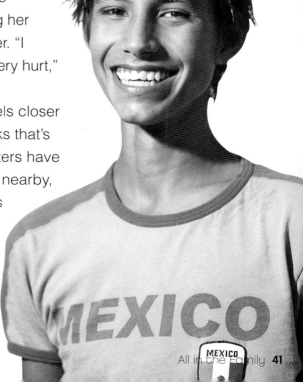

Today, Jamie feels closer to Michel. But he thinks that's because his older sisters have moved out. Vera lives nearby, and they go to movies together a lot. Occasionally, he sleeps over at her house. Lorin lives in Massachusetts, and he misses her a lot. The two of them share a similar sense of humor and taste in music.

Jamie has a lot of respect for Vera and Lorin, despite his dangerous descent from the second floor. He says he never thinks of them as anything less than true sisters. "A half sibling," he says, "is simply a sibling."

About Half Siblings

Half siblings are brothers or sisters who share one biological parent but not the other. It's hard to say how many kids in the United States have half siblings. What we do know is that about 30 percent of American kids—more than 20 million in all—live with a stepparent.

In many of these **stepfamilies**, the parents decide to have new children together. These new additions to the family are called **mutual children** because they are biologically related to both parents. The children from their parents' previous relationships are their half siblings.

Are half siblings really no different from **full siblings**, as Jamie says? According to Anne C. Bernstein, a family psychologist in Berkeley, California,

it's often more complicated than that. Unlike their half siblings, she says, mutual children "haven't had to deal with their parents separating, divorcing, or dying, so they haven't had those losses to process." They also haven't had to learn to live with a stepparent. And while Jamie resented his older sisters' special vacations, it often works the other way around. Older siblings can get jealous of their mutual siblings' blood ties to both parents.

TIPS
for Half
SIBS

LOSE THE LABELS: According to Bernstein, Jamie is right to think of his siblings as sisters, not half sisters.

EXPRESS YOURSELF: If you feel as though your parents are playing favorites, speak up. But try to do it in a positive way. Keep the focus on how you're feeling rather than on what they're doing wrong.

THE GRASS ISN'T GREENER: Don't imagine that your life would be better if your family were simpler. "People tend to have rather idealized views of what their lives would be like if they didn't live in a stepfamily," says Bernstein.

Mutual children face their own challenges, however. Parents often see them as the glue that will help bind the new family. "The promise of having 'one that is ours' is that he will tie together fragments of two families and make them one," says Bernstein. Mutual children may feel it is their responsibility to keep everyone happy. That's a lot of pressure for one kid to bear.

BY THE
numbers

Judging from divorce statistics, more American kids have been getting used to blended families over the past 50 years.

The number of divorces per 1,000 Americans went from 2.6 in 1950 to 3.6 in 2005. (It reached a high of 5.3 around 1980.)

Seventy-five percent of the people who divorce will remarry.

75%

About 63 percent of Americans grow up with both biological parents.

63%

Middle
SIBS

Liam's Story

At 16, Liam is quick to point out that he is not the baby of his family. He does have two older siblings: Dylan, who is 21; and Cate, who is 23. But his 14-year-old brother Macklin is definitely the youngest. The trouble, according to Liam, is that no one else sees it that way.

Liam claims he has always had to follow the same rules as Macklin, despite their two-year age difference. Family vacations are his biggest complaint. As far back as he can remember, Dylan and Cate got to stay home if they wanted to. Liam and Macklin had no choice. Every year, they were force-marched to the beach or the ski slopes—even though Liam hated skiing.

Liam admits that his status as a younger sibling has its advantages. "My older sister and brother had special chores, like washing the dishes," Liam says. "I must have washed the dishes like four times since I don't know when. Same goes for my younger brother." Liam is quick to add that he does have more chores than Macklin—yet they don't earn him the respect that his older siblings get from his parents.

In many ways, Liam feels stuck in the middle. His parents don't put much pressure on him, he says. But he feels he has to work hard to carve out an identity. "You have the man of the house above you and the younger kid below you, so you have to try to stand out," he explains.

Liam makes his mark by doing well in school, which hasn't been a strength for either of his brothers. "I'm not one of the kids who are quiet and sit in the back of the classroom," he says. "I try to be deliberately outspoken."

Like a lot of middle children, Liam seems to have learned diplomacy from balancing both younger and older siblings. He considers himself friends with about half the kids at his high school, and he rarely has conflicts with any of them. Maybe there are advantages to being the (almost) baby after all!

About Middle Sibs

According to psychologist Kevin Leman, middle children tend to grow up outside the spotlight. They don't have the burden of expectations felt by the oldest child. And they don't command the attention that younger siblings do. When they reach the same milestones as their older siblings—like speaking or walking for the first time—parents may not be as impressed as they were the first time around. Leman's opinion is that all these factors can conspire to make middle children insecure.

But if you believe the birth-order theorists, getting sandwiched between siblings can be a big advantage. Middle children have to make alliances in the family in order to get their way, using skills that can serve them well outside the house. According to Leman, middle children are "relational by nature." They make loyal friends, good listeners, and expert **mediators**. They also tend to do well in team sports.

Tips for
middle sibs

APPRECIATE YOUR STRENGTHS. Thinking about the effects of birth order might help you uncover some of your strong points. According to Leman: "You thrive on friendships. You are inherently a good listener, and one of your main personality skills that makes you so lovable is that you're loyal."

DON'T BOX YOURSELF IN. Be forewarned that birth-order theory is made up of a lot of broad generalizations. Your personality is the result of many factors, not just your relative age in the family.

by the
numbers

Because of lower birth rates, middle children now take up a smaller portion of the population than they have in the past.

From the late 1950s to 2005, the average number of kids born to each woman in the United States dropped from 3.8 to 2.1.

The percentage of American households with five or more people dropped from 20 percent in 1970 to 11 percent in 2000.

FAMOUS
middle sibs

Susan B. Anthony, women's rights activist

Steve Forbes, publisher and politician

Bill Gates, Microsoft founder

Jay Leno, talk show host

Donald Trump, real estate developer

Barbara Walters, TV journalist

Oldest
SIBS

Elizabeth's Story

Elizabeth was five years old when her mother came home from the hospital with her baby brother, Kevin. "My mom told me that he was my baby," she remembers, "not that I had given birth to him, but that she had brought him home almost as a present for me."

It didn't take long before the novelty wore off. Elizabeth remembers a couple of years of peace with Kevin. Then she began to feel like he was replacing her. Her father started taking her to skating lessons because her mom didn't have the time. He didn't do things exactly the way her mother did, and he was usually late. She missed the time with her mom. It didn't help that her best friend was an only child who didn't have to share her parents with anyone. Elizabeth started to wonder, "Why aren't I getting as much attention at home as she gets?"

Now Elizabeth is in tenth grade, and the issues have changed. Her parents pressure her to get good grades, while Kevin sails through fifth grade without that stress. Sometimes her mom and dad make her baby-sit for Kevin when she'd rather be out with her friends. They also expect her to set a good example for her younger brother.

Elizabeth takes it all pretty much in stride. She even sounds proud of her role as an older sister. "I kind of teach Kevin how to be a better person, how to handle stress, and how to behave around people—social skills and stuff," she says. Elizabeth has friends whose older siblings are pretty wild. With that in mind, she tries to stay away from parties where people are drinking—"for myself," she says, "but also for Kevin."

Over the years, Elizabeth has discovered she has a lot of affection for her little brother. Sometimes when her friends come over, he'll dance around or crank up the radio. She thinks it's funny, even though her friends find it annoying. She also claims that Kevin teaches her more than she teaches him. "He knows every animal by its Latin name," she says. "He could probably help me with my math homework, and I'm in honors math."

Elizabeth still feels jealous that she has to share her mom's attention with her brother. But the age and gender differences help a lot, she says. She and Kevin aren't going through the same things at the same time. And, most important, they don't have to fight over clothes. "We're our own people," Elizabeth says. "We accept each other's differences and doing so makes us closer."

a **special** sib

JONATHAN, 16, IS THE OLDER BROTHER of Timmy, six, who has **Down syndrome**. That's a set of traits caused by a hereditary abnormality. Some physical features of Down syndrome are oval-shaped eyes, a flattened nasal bridge, a small mouth, and small ears. Someone with the syndrome is likely to be short and may gain weight easily. At least 50 percent suffer from heart defects, and between 60 to 80 percent have vision and hearing problems. People with Down syndrome have some degree of mental retardation.

Jonathan makes a point of trying not to treat Timmy differently. "You just have to accept that he is a bit slower than others," says Jonathan. "Sometimes I help him get dressed and help him with his homework. But I treat him like I would treat anyone."

Jonathan admits that Timmy's condition tests his ability to stay calm. When Jonathan gets irritated with Timmy's slowness, he wants to yell. But he has taught himself not to lose his temper, though it can be hard.

His brother has taught him to be patient, Jonathan says. He gets frustrated and upset when Timmy doesn't listen. "If you tell him something once, he just won't listen. But you just have to deal with it, and that's what teaches you patience."

Most of all, though, Timmy inspires his older brother. "He's fun-loving and sensitive," says Jonathan. "He's always happy. If someone asks me about my brother, I just explain how happy he is and how he just makes me laugh. He inspires me every day."

About Oldest Sibs

According to psychologists, Elizabeth's experience with Kevin's birth is typical. Firstborns usually have the full attention of their parents until a sibling comes around to "dethrone" them. Suddenly, their lives are turned upside down. They used to spend hours reading and playing with Mom and Dad; now they get to sit and watch while their little "present" is fed, changed, and snuggled to sleep. After the initial tantrums, most firstborns have one dominant reaction: They work harder to please their parents.

BY THE numbers

Are firstborns really smarter and more successful than their younger siblings? Well, maybe.

Most American presidents have been firstborns or firstborn boys in their families.

In a Norwegian study of more than 240,000 men, the IQs of firstborn siblings were two points higher on average than those of later-borns.

The strategies they use to win back parental attention, according to birth-order theorists, shape their personalities for life. The one thing firstborns have over their younger siblings is competence. At least in the early years, they're better at everything: walking, reading, math, playing the piano. They learn quickly that achievement in these areas wins praise from their parents. Parents grow to expect the best out of their oldest—and firstborns often respond, turning into serious, hardworking adults. Kevin Leman, in *The Birth Order Book*, writes that firstborns "are more highly motivated to achieve than later-borns." Many, according to Leman, go on to become leaders—ministers, CEOs, even presidents.

FAMOUS
oldest sibs

George W. Bush, U.S. president

Bill Cosby, comedian

Hillary Rodham Clinton, U.S. senator

Oprah Winfrey, TV host and media mogul

TIPS
for Oldest
SIBS

QUESTION YOUR ROLE:
If you feel pressured to succeed or be responsible beyond your years, bring it up with your parents. "Don't rebel or argue," says Richard Gallagher of the New York University Child Study Center. "Discuss whether you are expected to do much more than the other kids in your family."

BACK OFF: Firstborns love to tell people what to do, according to Kevin Leman. But just because you have high expectations for yourself doesn't mean you should impose them on others.

KEEP PERSPECTIVE: High-achievers can get single-minded about their goals. It doesn't hurt to relax and make sure you have balance in your life.

Only KIDS

Natalie's Story

As an only child, Natalie has to rely on friends for an education in the joys of brotherly and sisterly love. She knows one girl whose little brother lives to insult her. Other households seem to be in a perpetual state of war. Siblings fight constantly over their share of food or money. After a few visits around her Rhode Island neighborhood, Natalie's occasional bouts with loneliness don't seem so bad. "I don't mean to sound selfish," she says, "but I enjoy not having to share everything."

Maybe most of all, Natalie likes having her parents to herself. The family eats together often, and she loves the dinner-table conversations. She

likes going on trips with her mom—to the mall, the movies, or even the zoo. With her dad she shares a love of ferry rides, music, and restaurants. "Being an only child has brought me and my parents closer than if I had siblings," she says.

Natalie cares a lot about what other people think of her—especially adults. She tries hard to get along with her teachers and earns nearly straight As in school. She plays soccer and runs track. Sometimes she pushes herself so hard that her parents have to tell her to relax. "My mom says that while I give 110 percent on everything, I can be too hard on myself," Natalie says.

17.4%
2004

9.6%
1976

BY THE numbers

Only children may feel lonely sometimes, but these days their numbers are increasing fast. Why? Women with full-time careers are waiting longer to get pregnant and having fewer children once they do.

In 1976, 9.6 percent of women between the ages of 40 and 44 had only one child. In 2004, 17.4 percent had only one child.

Tips for
only kids

CUT EVERYONE SOME SLACK: Only kids can be even more critical than oldest sibs—of themselves and of other people. Try to lighten up.

FIGHT JEALOUSY: Since you never had to share your parents' attention, it may be hard for you to share your friends' attention as well. Remember that when friends show affection for others, it doesn't mean they like you less.

ALWAYS CONNECT: Relationships may not come naturally to you, but they are essential. Work hard to keep your friendships in good shape.

With only one child to raise, Natalie's parents take a strong interest in her life—sometimes too strong, according to Natalie. She says they worry about her too much and get "way too overprotective." They like their daughter to plan ahead, which makes it hard to have friends over on the spur of the moment. There are plenty of times when Natalie wishes she had companions her age living in her house.

When she gets lonely, though, Natalie has a solution. Instead of a sibling, she turns to her dog, Guinness. "Whenever I'm upset or sad, I snuggle with my dog," she says. "Sometimes when I want to run and play, I'll go outside and play ball with him. My dog is someone I can always count on to be there when I need him." And unlike a sibling, Guinness doesn't call Natalie names or fight with her over the size of his allowance!

About Only Children

Only children are often described as extreme versions of older siblings. They are firstborns, just like older sibs, and their parents invest a lot in them. According to Kevin Leman, that can turn them into superachievers. In the spotlight all the time at home, they often feel great pressure to succeed. Many only children, like Natalie, can grow up to be highly self-critical.

Only children spend a lot of time by themselves or with their parents, and that can also

Only children tend to be very independent.

have a big effect on their lives. They tend to be very independent, and they're often described as "mature for their age." Like Natalie, they may prefer the company of adults.

For Natalie, the loneliness of not having siblings is balanced by the fact that she never has to compete for food, attention, or money. But this can have its drawbacks as well. Outside the home, people compete for grades, jobs, space in a college dorm room, and lots of other things. Only children often struggle to learn how to join the fray.

FAMOUS
only children

Elizabeth Bishop, poet

Sarah Michelle Gellar, actor

Rudolph Giuliani, politician

William Randolph Hearst, newspaper publisher

Elton John, pop star

Tommy Lee Jones, actor

Natalie Portman, actor

Frank Sinatra, singer

Alexander Solzhenitsyn, author and dissident

Step-SIBLINGS

Lexi's Story

It is often challenging for kids when their parents get divorced. They may miss living in the same home with both biological parents. Visiting schedules can be tough. But for Lexi, 15, the most difficult adjustment was not her parents' divorce. It was her dad's second marriage—and the step-siblings who came along with it.

Lexi's dad remarried six years ago. His new wife, Debbie, brought with her a 13-year-old daughter named Jennifer and a ten-year-old son named Eric. Lexi is not happy about the new arrivals. "I think my life was fine without step-siblings," Lexi says. "I hardly see my dad anymore, so I feel like they have replaced me. I always feel left out."

"I always feel left out."

Lexi and her biological brother, Connor, spend most of their time at their mother's house in California. One night each weekend, they sleep at their dad's house, about ten minutes away.

For Lexi, it's a hard transition. "My stepmom is very strict and has a lot of unneeded rules, like about what we have to drink for dinner," she says. "That is something my mom would never care about."

Lexi says her stepmom favors Jennifer and Eric over Lexi and Connor. "Whenever something goes wrong, it's usually my fault," she says. To stay out of trouble, Lexi has learned to avoid picking fights with her step-siblings. She's much more comfortable speaking her mind with Connor, even though they only get along about "half the time."

Lexi is not sure how she feels about her living arrangement. She's grateful that she only has to share a house with her step-siblings once a week. "It is good to have my own space to relax and not feel like I'm always around them," she says. But she can't help being envious of the time they spend with her father.

Even though Lexi struggles to get along with her step-siblings, she would advise other kids that it's worth making the effort. "You'll be around them enough that you'll want to have a good relationship with them," she says.

About Step-Siblings

Lexi may sometimes feel like a stranger in her own family. But she's not alone. Experts estimate that six out of ten American kids will live in a stepfamily at some point in their lives.

"You'll be around your step-siblings enough that you'll want to have a good relationship with them."

TIPS for step SIBS

BE TOGETHER: It takes effort for stepfamilies to build strong relationships. Make plans to do things together, even if you don't always feel like it. Go to sporting events or movies, play board games, and try to eat meals as a family.

BE APART: Make sure you get some time alone with your biological parent, says Jeannette Lofas, founder of the Stepfamily Foundation. You need to be able to share your feelings with your dad or mom without anyone else around.

ESTABLISH RULES: Try to get your parent and stepparent to set clear rules in the house. According to Lofas, it's easy to get confused and fail to communicate when you're shuttling from house to house.

Like Lexi, many of these kids are forced to adapt to a whole new set of household rules. "Two different family cultures are coming together," says Charlotte Shoup Olsen, who teaches family studies at Kansas State University. "One family may have a sit-down meal; the other family may be used to eating in front of the TV. One family may be used to having every person participate in the housecleaning, while the other may not expect the children to do too much."

In the beginning, stepchildren are often mourning the end of their parents' marriage and may be reluctant to embrace their new stepfamily. Add to that fresh competition for a parent's attention from a set of new step-siblings. It can take a long time for the two sides to lay down their resentment and become friends.

by the
NUMBERS

Due to a high divorce rate, more Americans may live in stepfamilies than in nuclear families.

Nearly **one million divorces** are finalized in the United States each year; that's about one for every 2.3 new marriages.

About **75 percent** of people who divorce remarry.

75%

65%

About **65 percent** of remarriages involve children from previous marriages; this makes for about 1,300 new stepfamilies a day.

FAMOUS
stepchildren

Elizabeth I, queen of England

Jane Fonda, actor

Abraham Lincoln, U.S. president

Shaquille O'Neal, four-time NBA champion

Nancy Reagan, first lady

Twin
SIBS

Amy and Ashly's Story

Amy and Ashly remember it like it was yesterday. It was the longest the 16-year-old identical twins from San Antonio, Texas, have ever spent apart. Was it a month? A week? No, it was a single night! "It happened in the third grade. I got invited to a sleep-over birthday party and Ashly didn't," says Amy. "It was really, really, really weird."

These days, Amy and Ashly make a point to be apart as little as possible. "We just want to be with each other," says Amy.

"We have a better time when we're together," Ashly adds. "Our parents ask us if we want to do different things, but we don't. When Amy's away, I don't feel quite complete."

Amy and Ashly look almost exactly alike. People who know them can tell them apart because Amy has more freckles on her face. They act alike, too. They both play golf. They have the same friends. "Every single friend," Ashly adds. "We share them."

The twins do almost identically well in school—and they do best when they are in the same classes. "We get higher grades when we're together, and we don't know why," says Ashly. "Third grade is the year we were separated, and we did really badly in school that year."

That doesn't mean they don't run into trouble in the classroom. Once, they got exactly the same questions wrong on a test. "The teacher had a conference with us and asked us if we had cheated," Ashly says. "We hadn't. It actually happens quite a bit—missing the same questions—even when we're not in classes together."

The amazing bond between twins, especially identical twins, can make it hard for outsiders. Amy and Ashly say some of their friends have become jealous of their ultra-close relationship.

Right now, though, the girls can't imagine anyone coming between them. They're planning to go to the same college. When they graduate, they want to become beauticians and open a salon together. After that, both girls say they'd like to marry twin brothers. "That would be cool," says Amy. "They wouldn't be jealous of the bond we have, and they'd know how it feels to want to be with your twin."

About Twins

Amy and Ashly are not unusual, according to Nancy L. Segal, director of the Twin Studies Center at California State University, Fullerton. Segal, who wrote *Entwined Lives: Twins and What They Tell Us About Human Behavior*, says that twins tend to be "very similar on most traits—personality, intelligence, interests, even how quickly or slowly they fall in love."

The intense closeness that twins develop can be a burden at times. "Most teenagers tend to question their identity and explore who they are in relation to others," says Segal. "Twins may feel guilty if one wants to explore more than the other."

It's important to treat twins as individuals, Segal says, but that does not mean forcing them to separate if they don't want to. Amy and Ashly claim that they do better in school when they're together, and research suggests that the same is true for other twins.

In general, Segal thinks twins are lucky to have each other. "Most people crave the kind of intimacy twins have so naturally," she says. "I think twins should enjoy what they have and make the most of it. It's an extremely special relationship."

"Most people crave the kind of intimacy twins have so naturally."

TYPES OF TWINS

THERE ARE TWO TYPES OF TWINS:

FRATERNAL AND IDENTICAL

FRATERNAL TWINS are created when two eggs in the mother's body are fertilized separately. They are really just siblings who happen to have the same birthday. IDENTICAL TWINS develop from a single egg that splits in two. Identical twins have identical DNA, the genetic material that determines many aspects of our physical development. Basically, at birth, identical twins are natural-born clones. One thing fraternal and identical twins have in common: most of the time these pairs grow up together in the same environment.

TIPS
for
TWINS

STRIKE A BALANCE: Enjoy the bond that you have, but give each other the space to be different. If one twin is more adventurous than the other, that's fine. Try not to hold each other back.

BE SENSITIVE TO OTHER SIBLINGS: Twins command a lot of attention. It's easy for a non-twin sibling to feel ignored and excluded. Try to include other siblings and give them room to shine.

BEWARE OF JEALOUSY: Twins often tend to like the same kinds of people, says Segal. When you start dating, that can create problems.

BY THE
numbers

If you think you're seeing double these days, you may be right. More and more women are having twins, thanks to the increased use of fertility drugs, which raise the chance of multiple births. Here are some facts about twins.

Between 1980 and 2000, the twin birth rate rose by nearly 50 percent.

In 2003, 3.1 percent of all births in the United States were twins.

Fraternal twins are twice as likely as non-twins to have twin children.

Twins are twice as likely as non-twins to be left-handed.

FAMOUS
twins

Ronde and Tiki Barber, NFL football players

Bob and Mike Bryan, ATP pro tennis players

Barbara and Jenna Bush, daughters of President
  George W. Bush

Ann Landers and Abigail Van Buren,
  advice columnists

Brian and Brandon Casey, R & B artists (from
  Jagged Edge)

Mary-Kate and Ashley Olsen, actors

Youngest
SIBS

Jenny's Story

Ever since she was seven years old, Jenny has wanted to hang out with her older brother, Andrew, and his friends. Sometimes Andrew let her, and Jenny happily joined the war games or took a turn with the video game controller. Sometimes he excluded her, and she vented her frustration by trying to beat him up. One way or the other, she was determined to be the center of attention. "I often crave the spotlight," says Jenny, who is now 15. "I just like people being able to notice me and know what I'm doing."

The way Jenny tells it, it probably isn't hard to compete with Andrew for attention. Andrew has always been quiet by nature. He doesn't mind being alone for hours at a time, reading or hanging out in his room. Jenny, who is almost two years younger, wasted no time carving out a distinct personality for herself. She loves making her friends laugh and needs constant activity to be happy. "If I'm not doing something, I'm just miserable all day," she says.

Even though Andrew doesn't get outside much, he casts a pretty long shadow in Jenny's life. She complains that her parents compare her to her older brother too often. "They always say, 'Well, your brother got this grade and you should be doing that as well,'" she says. Even his failures seem to have an effect on her life. Her parents don't want her to take European history because Andrew didn't do well in it last year.

Andrew doesn't mind playing the role of the wiser, more experienced older brother. According to Jenny, she takes a lot of his advice, but he doesn't always listen when she tries to return the favor. "Even though we're only 22 months apart, he'll try to come off as if he knows more about what he's talking about than I do."

But in one very important way, Jenny and Andrew have become equals. Andrew is now happy to include Jenny when his friends are around. In fact, he doesn't have much of a choice. "A lot of our friends are friends with each other," Jenny says. One of Andrew's best friends even came close to dating one of Jenny's friends.

"I will certainly miss having a friend around 24/7."

At home, brother and sister have forged an alliance. They talk to each other about problems in their lives. They've made a pact to keep incriminating secrets from their parents. They back each other up in family fights with their mom or dad. Jenny is already thinking about how hard it will be to watch Andrew go off to college. "I will certainly miss having a friend around 24/7," she says.

About Youngest Sibs

Youngest children might feel that they get no respect. In the heat of family competition, their brothers and sisters may treat them like babies. Parents and other adults may think of them as less competent than their siblings. (In many cases, they are—they're younger, after all.)

But don't underestimate last-borns. According to birth-order theories, these kids have an effective way to fight back. Since they can't seem to get attention for their accomplishments, they often become entertainers. Jenny is a good example. Faced with a serious, hardworking older brother, she learned how to draw a crowd by making people laugh.

Last-borns also tend to be rebels, says Frank J. Sulloway, author of *Born to Rebel: Birth Order, Family Dynamics, and Creative Lives*. Older kids tend to identify with authority, scolding their younger siblings for not following the rules. Youngest kids often feel like the rules are stacked against them and that they have nothing to lose by breaking them. In fact, acting out can get them the attention they crave. According to Sulloway, many last-borns put their rebellious nature to use later in life. They become risk takers and make their mark as activists or creative artists.

FAMOUS
youngest children

Drew Carey, comedian and game show host

Jim Carrey, actor and comedian

Billy Crystal, actor and comedian

Rosie O'Donnell, actor and TV host

Whoopi Goldberg, actor and comedian

Michael Phelps, Olympic swimmer

Ronald Reagan, actor and U.S. president

Roy Williams, college and Olympic basketball coach

Tips for
youngest kids

ASK FOR RESPECT: Don't be afraid to gently let people know when they're not giving you credit for your accomplishments.

DON'T MANIPULATE: You probably know exactly how to get an older brother or sister in trouble, says Kevin Leman. That tendency to manipulate people may work in the short term, but over time it will earn you enemies.

DON'T DUCK RESPONSIBILITIES: You may be good at making excuses and avoiding trouble, says Leman, but taking responsibility for your actions will serve you better in the long run.

USE YOUR CHARM: There are a lot of jobs out there that require great people skills. Be proud of yours and use them wisely.

family
feuds

family feuds

I JUST TRY TO LEAVE HIM ALONE

"Kevin and I fight when I touch his stuff. He doesn't like that. Also, a lot of times we'll start playing, physical play, and then he'll get hurt and he'll say I'm being mean to him. Usually I just try to leave him alone after a fight because he's the kind of person who won't really reason with you."

—Elizabeth, 15

"When we were younger, Andrew and I used to fight a lot. We would beat each other up like kids tend to do. I would hit him if I was mad at him for not letting me play games with him and his friends, or for insisting on watching a TV show I didn't want to watch. Eventually we would just get over our fights or get in time-outs and have to say sorry."

—Jenny, 15

"[Macklin and I] don't really like each other. [He] does not share anything, and he gets really mad if you touch any of his stuff. Anytime I touch his lacrosse stick, he goes ballistic. We slap each other around, punch a couple times. But nothing really serious."

—Liam, 16

Why Can't We All Just Get Along?

Elizabeth, Jenny, Liam, and most of the other teens profiled in this book have one thing in common: they love their siblings—and hate them. To outsiders, it may seem shocking how eager siblings can be to beat each other into submission. (Think of only-child Natalie's reaction to the power struggles in her friends' homes.)

But experts say that they can't help it—brothers and sisters were born to battle over everything from table scraps to test scores. "Siblings compete over status in the family or just status in general," says Linda Dunlap, head of the psychology department at Marist College in Poughkeepsie, New York. "They compare themselves on just about anything—how well they do in school, how attractive they are, how many friends they have."

Sibling rivalry is so widespread that many people think of it as an instinct, bred into species over millions of years. Consider what still happens in the wild. Most birds establish a "pecking order" in which the strongest chicks get all the food and

their weaker siblings starve. Some birds—as well as sharks, amphibians, and other animals—take their rivalry a step further. The weaker brothers and sisters actually become lunch!

Given that backdrop, bickering over the TV remote sounds pretty tame. But Frank Sulloway says that the same principle is involved. "Remember that 200 years ago, half of all children did not survive childhood," says Sulloway. Human beings are built to fight for "all the resources that get you out of childhood alive," he says. "But our genes don't know that we are living in a different world."

Fight and Learn

In the moment, sibling rivalry can seem painful, exhausting, or just plain annoying. It may, however, be preparing you to deal with conflict for years to come. Day after day, brothers and sisters get to test their skills in the heat of battle. Since they share the same home, it's hard to run away from conflict. And siblings can be pretty honest with each other without risking their relationship. "The sibling relationship is a pretty safe place to try things out, to be competitive, to argue," says Dunlap. "Why? Because your sibling is probably the most likely person to ultimately forgive you."

It's easy to spot this resilience in Jenny, Elizabeth, and Liam. None of them seem to hold grudges against their siblings. Jenny and Andrew suffered through their time-outs, Jenny says; then they

"The sibling relationship is a pretty safe place to try things out, to be competitive, to argue."

"would just forgive and forget." Elizabeth gives Kevin a little space to get over his anger; then they pick up where they left off. "We don't usually say we're sorry," she says. "We just assume we're over it when we start playing again." Even Liam dismisses his boxing matches with Macklin as "nothing really serious."

Competition that doesn't end in bloody noses or broken bones can also spur us on to greater achievements. A lazy student who finds out his sister got straight As, for example, might be inspired to do better in school. But Dunlap says teens need to discover this kind of motivation by themselves. Parents who say things like "Why can't you make good grades like your sister?" usually fail to improve anyone's study habits. Comparing yourself constantly to an older brother or sister can wreck your self-esteem and steer you down paths that aren't right for you.

FIRST AID
for Sibling Combatants

✚ **TALK TO YOUR SIBLING.** "The difference between a healthy family and an unhealthy family is the extent to which the people in the family are able to communicate," says Neil Talkoff, a psychologist at the San Francisco Psychoanalytic Institute and Society.

✚ **TRY TIME APART.** Some conflicts arise out of basic personality differences. When an introvert like Andrew has to live with an extrovert like Jenny, sparks are bound to fly. It can help to give each other some space, the way Elizabeth and Kevin do.

✚ **CELEBRATE YOUR UNIQUENESS.** Chances are you wouldn't want to be a clone of your siblings, no matter what they've accomplished. "There are some things that our siblings will be good at and other things that [you] will be good at," Linda Dunlap says. "Find ways to feel confident about yourself where you don't have to compare yourself to anyone else."

+ DON'T INSIST THAT EVERYTHING BE EQUAL.
Try not to count every privilege doled out in the
family. "Different people have different needs, and
parents do their best to recognize and fulfill those
needs," says Dunlap. "What's important is not who's
getting more, but that what each sibling is getting is
sufficient. Get over it."

+ SOLVE THE PROBLEM. Both you and your sibling
have brains. Use them to solve disputes rather than
getting trapped in a power struggle. Say you always
fight about who gets to sit in the front seat of the
car. Try alternating each week.

+ GET SOME PERSPECTIVE. Chances are you won't
always hate your brother or sister. Siblings who
can't stand each other in grade school often turn
out to be the best of friends once they leave home.

+ GET ADULT HELP. Sometimes you need a mediator.
Dunlap suggests family meetings to help resolve
especially difficult conflicts.

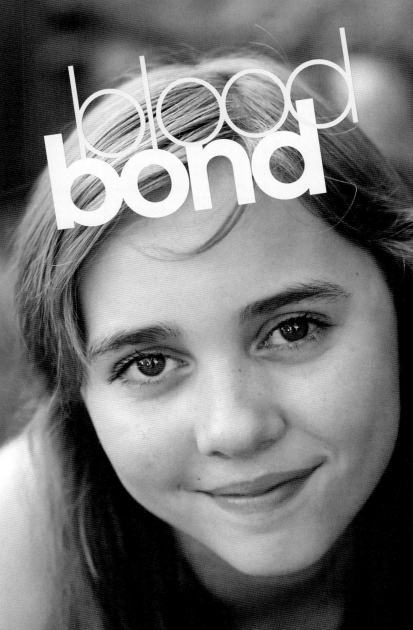

blood
bond

blood bond

"I'M GOING TO BE THERE FOR HIM WHEN HE NEEDS ME."

Cindy's Story

When I was in third grade, I moved with my family from Colombia to the United States. My brother, Guillermo, was five. It was very hard and very scary. I didn't know [anyone], just my uncle. I had to go into a new school. I didn't know the language, so I couldn't even communicate with people. I didn't say anything at first except "hi" and "okay."

Guillermo was supposed to be in first grade, but they left him back to kindergarten since he didn't know English. I was learning more advanced stuff with the writing, and he was learning how to spell words. So we helped each other. We both didn't know [anything], so whatever we knew we would tell each other. By fourth grade, I was already getting B honor rolls and by fifth grade A honor rolls. I was really happy I adjusted [quickly] and did well in school.

Since Guillermo is obviously younger, I feel he's not as mature as me. He'll do little stuff like start jumping around when I'm trying to watch TV, and sometimes it kind of gets to me.

But he can be a lot of fun, too. I'll play video games with him and learn because I'm not as good as he is. At the end of the day, he's my brother, and I'm going to be there for him when he needs me.

It's very important to me that we stay close. Even if we don't live

in the same city when we're older, we should call each
other and visit each other and help each other out.
Hopefully we will have a good future, and our parents'
sacrifices will be worth it.

—Cindy, 15

Cindy and Guillermo have been through a lot together. They moved to a new country where they didn't know anyone and didn't speak the language. They had to learn to communicate, find friends, and catch up in school. The experience didn't completely erase their differences; Guillermo still manages to drive his older sister crazy. But those differences faded in the face of the challenges they dealt with together. When it counted most, they were there for each other. In most sibling relationships, that kind of alliance goes hand in hand with all the battles over TV time and parental attention. And this confusing mix of emotions is what the sibling bond is all about.

Few of the brothers and sisters in this book have had their lives dislocated as severely as Cindy and Guillermo. But many have come close. Skye and James had to leave their home and rely on two different sets of foster parents. Elizabeth and Kevin, Lexi and Connor—both sibling pairs lived through their parents' divorces.

You probably have shared plenty of experiences with your siblings. And this won't stop when you leave home. Other relationships will form and break up. Nephews and nieces will be born. Parents may get sick and need care. Through all of this, the most constant thing in your life may well be the presence of a brother or a sister.

When it counted most, they were there for each other.

You shouldn't assume that all the disputes and resentments just melt away as you age. Brothers and sisters find plenty to fight about as adults. But the accumulation of shared experience carries a powerful weight. Only your siblings will remember what it was like to wake up together on holiday mornings or welcome a new dog into the family. Many people find, both as kids and adults, that they can be more honest with their siblings than with anyone else. There's nothing you can say, after all, that will make your brother stop being your brother. And as time goes on, that makes the sibling bond seem pretty important. As psychiatrist Ruth Waldbaum says, "The need for family overrides all things."

Sound
OFF

Here are some raves about supportive siblings.

I have always had great people to look up to, like my sister and my mom. They are such big influences in my life.

—*Hilary Duff, 18, on sister Haylie, 21, as reported in* OK! *magazine*

Having a sister means I always have someone to talk to and lean on.

—*Actor Malcolm David Kelley of the TV show* Lost

How can I say it— she's just very smart. She really knows what's going on. She gets life. She means more than anything to me.

—*Joseph, 18, on his twin sister Christine*

I try to be a role model for him. We have a pretty good relationship. We never really fight. We kind of understand each other, but we don't hang out. We have a bond. I'd do anything for him.

—*Kristi, 19, on her younger brother Craig, 16*

Aly and I are a total team. We're best friends and can really talk and make decisions together.

—*AJ Michalka, 16, on sister Aly, 18, as reported in J-14 magazine*

I think it's cool that I have someone who shares many genes with me. It's cool that I have someone that will always be on my side. It makes me work extra hard on having us on good terms. I love that when I get older and both my parents are gone, I'll still have him.

—*Elizabeth, 15, on her younger brother Kevin, 10*

I think the best part about having a sister is that it's very inspiring. If I see her do well or I see her and she doesn't win a match, I'm always inspired and motivated by her, more than anyone else ever.

—*Venus Williams, 25, on sister Serena, 24, as reported in* OK! *magazine*

As my brother and I matured, we just realized how lucky we are to be so close in age. We're lucky to have someone to talk to and not have to worry about being judged. I have my best friend and he has his, but sometimes it's not as easy to talk to them about certain things.

—*Jenny, 15, on her older brother Andrew, who is almost 17*

adolescent—someone who is in the teenage years between childhood and adulthood

biological—connected by direct genetic relationship rather than by adoption or marriage

birth order—where a person falls in age as compared to his or her siblings

Down syndrome—an inherited disorder that causes slight mental retardation and physical abnormalities

extrovert—someone who is outgoing

foster care—a system in which trained and licensed adults take in youths who are unable to live with their biological parents

full siblings—brothers and sisters who have the same biological parents

half siblings—brothers and sisters who share one biological parent but not the other

interact—to act together in a way that affects each other

introvert—someone who is turned inward; shy

mediators—people who work to get two parties to compromise

mutual children—kids who are born into a stepfamily

nuclear families—groups of two parents and their children, all living in the same home with no other relatives

personalities—people's mental, emotional, and social characteristics

psychiatrist—a medical doctor trained to diagnose and treat mental disorders

psychologist—someone who studies people's minds and emotions and the ways people behave

relationships—connections between people

sibling rivalry—competition or animosity among brothers and sisters

siblings—two or more individuals having one common parent

stepfamilies—families made up of a parent, stepparent, and any children from a previous relationship

Books

Block, Joel D. and Susan Bartell. *Stepliving for Teens: Getting Along with Stepparents, Parents, and Siblings.* New York: Price Stern Sloan, 2001.

Cohen, Shari. *Coping with Sibling Rivalry.* New York: The Rosen Publishing Group, Inc., 1989.

Gottlieb, Andrew R. *Side by Side: On Having a Gay or Lesbian Sibling.* New York: Harrington Park Press, 2005.

Leman, Kevin. *The New Birth Order Book: Why You Are the Way You Are.* Old Tappan, NJ: Fleming H. Revell, 1998.

Meyer, Don. *The Sibling Slam Book: What It's Really Like to Have a Brother or Sister with Special Needs.* Bethesda, MD: Woodbine House, Inc., 2005.

Sulloway, Frank J. *Born to Rebel: Birth Order, Family Dynamics, and Creative Lives.* New York: Pantheon Books, 1996.

Online Sites & Organizations

Big Brothers Big Sisters
www.bbbs.org
The country's oldest and largest youth mentoring organization. High school students can volunteer for school-based mentoring programs, serving as big brothers or sisters to younger children.

The Center for Adoption Support and Education, Inc.
www.adoptionsupport.org/res/teens.html
Includes advice for adopted teens on dealing with a wide range of emotions, from anger to loneliness. Also includes a list of famous adoptees and an organizer for teens to create a personal portrait.

FosterClub
www.fosterclub.com
A nonprofit organization that educates youth in foster care, encouraging them to share experiences and enter contests. The engaging Web site includes an activity to make a scrapbook of your life, foster care facts and statistics, and an area just for teens.

National Stepfamily Resource Center
www.stepfamilies.info
Provides information, resources, and support to stepfamily members and professionals who work with them.

Parents, Families and Friends of Lesbians and Gays
www.pflag.org
An organization that offers support groups for people when a loved one declares his or her homosexuality.

Sibling Support Project
www.siblingsupport.org
A program designed to support people who have siblings with special needs. Organizes workshops, "Sibshops" (celebrations of the efforts of brothers and sisters of kids with special needs), and online support groups.

Stepfamily Foundation
www.stepfamily.org
An organization that offers articles, books, counseling, and other resources to support kids living in stepfamilies.

About the Author

Elizabeth Siris Winchester has been writing for children, teachers, and parents for the past ten years. As a writer and editor at *Time for Kids* magazine from 1999 to 2005, she covered everything from scientific discoveries and politics to bullying and dog shows. Liz is now a freelance writer and editor. Her published books include *The Right Bite: Dentists As Detectives* (Scholastic, 2007).

Liz thought a lot about her brother, John, as she worked on this book. He is two and a half years younger, but Liz says he is just as smart as she is, maybe even smarter! "Now a lawyer, John even reviewed my contract for this book," she says. From their earliest days, Liz and John fought constantly. John would use his weight ("He used to sit on me," she said) and strength to hurt Liz when she beat him at games. Her weapons were her wounding words. In spite of it all, the pair helped each other through difficult times, including their parents' divorce, and they remain close friends. "I often think that I wouldn't have survived childhood without John," Liz says.